Devraja Market, Mysore, India

How Much?

HarperCollins Publishers

Visiting Markets
Around the World
by Ted Lewin

arkets are found everywhere. They are found in dusty Egyptian deserts. They float on canals in Thailand. They bloom in the darkness of Indian flower stalls. They are even found in gravel parking lots. There is a market in the mountains of Peru with a train running through it. And there is a market in New Jersey where one person's junk becomes another's treasure.

Damnoen Saduak Floating Market,
near Bangkok, Thailand

Southwest of Bangkok, a spiderweb of small canals, or khlangs, flows into the main khlang. Just off it, small wooden boats, paddled mostly by women, nuzzle and bump their way into the floating market.

The boats carry children surrounded by mounds of coconuts, mangoes, pineapples, and less familiar fruits—pomelos, rambutans, longans, and tasty durians with spiky skins and a foul smell. Eating a durian is like eating vanilla custard in an outhouse.

On the fried-banana boat, the seller dips a banana into flour paste. Throws it into a steaming pot of boiling oil. Removes it and sprinkles coconut sugar on top. Pops it into a plastic bag. Delicious! And only twenty bahts (approximately fifty-three cents).

4

Around the bend, an elegant old woman rests
before she enters the busy marketplace.

Noise. Motor scooters and rickshaws, buses and bullock carts racing in the glaring sunlight.

Suddenly, the dark, stifling labyrinth of stalls takes over. Flower blossoms sporting brilliant colors burst from baskets illuminated by lamps hanging just above the heads of the flower sellers.

People are barely able to squeeze by one another in the narrow spaces. The ground is one foot deep in leaves, stems, and petals. Cut-green smell. White, orange, pink, and red flowers are sold by weight on balance scales. How much does a flower weigh?

The lamps reveal half a face here, a silhouetted hand, flashing white teeth there, half a body draped in a gorgeous silk sari.

Pilgrims on their way to Machu Picchu, the lost city of the Incas, stop at the marketplace in the valley below. Back and forth across the train tracks they shop for llama-wool ponchos and colorful textiles. An Indian woman sits on a plastic stool that straddles the tracks near her stall.

TOLDO PIZZA

With the mournful moan of the train's horn,
the ground trembles. The tracks vibrate. The train
rumbles into the market as children play only a few feet
away, oblivious to the danger. The woman picks up her plastic
stool and calmly moves to the side.

The train rattles on into the station. The woman returns to the tracks, and it's "back to business" . . . until the next train arrives.

At the camel market, the roofs of the low brick buildings are piled high
with hay—camel feed. The camels are hobbled so they can't stray far.
They're spray painted or branded for identification, like sheep or cattle.
And they're kept in check by cameleers wielding stout sticks.

"We've come all the way across the desert from Sudan.
It is a very long walk, my friend," says one weary cameleer.

Sticks thump. Camels bellow as they are herded into the compound. Mustafa, a buyer, sweeps inside. The bargaining begins. He examines each camel carefully, and then points to one with his whip. The deal is done. Has the camel been sold to Mustafa as a beast of burden or a pet? Or will it go to the slaughterhouse next door?

23

✳ Golden Nugget Antique and Collectible Flea Market, Lambertville, New Jersey

Three days every week, at 6 A.M., a parking lot in a New Jersey town transforms. Car trunks open like huge mouths disgorging the wonders of the universe onto big wooden tables—antiques, mostly new or broken, and collectibles not worth collecting.

"Just cleanin' out my attic," says a vendor selling ancient painted puppets from China, antique tools, hinges, and big brass letters. "I paid twenty-five dollars for the lot, and I get twenty-five dollars apiece now. You do the math," he says.

On the table sits a gray metal object the shape of brass knuckles, its use long forgotten.

"What is *that*?"

"Fifteen dollars, but I'll let it go for twelve," he replies.

Matt, age seven, began his career collecting action figures
when he was four, buying cheap at yard sales and selling
high at flea markets.

"The Putty People are hard to find," he explains.
Matt points to a five-inch-high winged demon.
"Goldar," he says reverently, "is *very* special."

37

♪ "Ethiopian" market,
Brooklyn, New York

Tao rai? [toe-RYE]

Enna velai? [ENN-uh vell-EYE]

Cuánto? [KWAN-toe]

Becaam? [bee-KAM]*

How much?

*Phonetic pronunciation for "How much?" in Thai, Tamil, Spanish, and Arabic

30

And so it goes in markets all over the world. No matter how you say it or where you say it, buying, selling, trading, and bargaining is a language we all understand.

✿ Pet market
under the highway,
Cairo, Egypt